GOBI DESERT

INNER MONGOLIA
AUTONOMOUS REGION

BEIJING
●BEIJING
Tianjin●
TIANJIN
Bohai
Sea

HEBEI

NINGXIA HUI
AUTONOMOUS
REGION

SHANXI

SHAANXI
Xi'an●

HENAN

SHANDONG

Yellow
River

Yellow River

Yellow
Sea

NORTH
KOREA

SOUTH
KOREA

Sea of
Japan
(East Sea)

JAPAN

JIANGSU

ANHUI
Nanjing●
Shanghai●
SHANGHAI

HEILONGJIANG

JILIN

LIAONING

HUBEI
Wuhan●

Yangtze River

CHONGQING

GUIZHOU

HUNAN

JIANGXI

ZHEJIANG

East
China
Sea

N

FUJIAN

Taipei●
TAIWAN

Tropic of Cancer

GUANGDONG
Guangzhou●

Pearl River

GUANGXI ZHUANG
AUTONOMOUS
REGION

Hong Kong
HONG KONG SPECIAL
ADMINISTRATIVE REGION
MACAU SPECIAL
ADMINISTRATIVE REGION

VIETNAM

Gulf of
Tonkin

HAINAN

South
China
Sea

PHILIPPINES

PACIFIC OCEAN

0   180   360   540 miles

Scale

CHINA

Land, Life, and Culture

People and Cities

JOHN AND JACKIE TIDEY

Marshall Cavendish
Benchmark
New York

This edition first published in 2009 in the United States of America by Marshall Cavendish Benchmark.

Marshall Cavendish Benchmark
99 White Plains Road
Tarrytown, NY 10591
www.marshallcavendish.us

All Internet sites were available and accurate when sent to press.

First published in 2008 by
MACMILLAN EDUCATION AUSTRALIA PTY LTD
15–19 Claremont Street, South Yarra 3141

Visit our website at www.macmillan.com.au or go directly to www.macmillanlibrary.com.au

Associated companies and representatives throughout the world.

Library of Congress Cataloging-in-Publication Data

Tidey, John.
    People and cities / by John and Jackie Tidey.
        p. cm. — (China: land, life and culture)
    Includes index.
    ISBN 978-0-7614-3158-9
    1. China—Social life and customs—2002---Juvenile literature.
    2. Cities and towns—China—Juvenile literature. I. Tidey, Jackie. II. Title.
    DS779.43.T54 2008
951—dc22

                                        2008002858

Edited by Georgina Garner
Text and cover design by Peter Shaw
Page layout by Peter Shaw
Photo research by Jes Senbergs
Maps by Damien Demaj, DEMAP
Illustration on p. 19 by Richard Morden

Printed in the United States

Acknowledgments
The author and the publisher are grateful to the following for permission to reproduce copyright material:

Cover photograph: Nanjing East Road, Shanghai, China, by Robert Harding World Imagery/Oriental Touch

Alamy, **19** (right); The Beijing Organizing Committee for the Games of the XXIX Olympiad **25** (bottom); Marion Ducco, **4** (top right), **5** (bottom), **20** (top), **23** (top), **30** (bottom); © Jacob/Dreamstime.com, **9** (bottom); DW Stock Picture Library, **6** (bottom), **11** (top); George Institute, **12**; Getty Images, **7**, **10** (bottom), **13** (bottom), **27** (top); Alex Headley, **11** (bottom), **27** (bottom); Juang Huamei, **14** (top); © istockphoto.com, **4** (bottom left); © Ying Chen/ istockphoto.com, **4** (bottom right); © Chandra Menard/iStockphoto, **28** (right); © Suprijono Suharjoto/istockphoto.com, **21** (top right); Robert Harding World Imagery/Oriental Touch **1**; Photolibrary/JTB Photo, **29** (top & bottom); © Shutterstock, **9** (top), **21**, (top left, middle left, middle right, bottom); © Max FX/Shutterstock, **4** (bottom middle); © Pieter Janssen/Shutterstock, **13** (middle); © Karin Lau/Shutterstock, **22** (bottom); © Tina Rencelj/Shutterstock, **19** (left); © Christophe Testi/Shutterstock, **28** (left), **30** (middle); © Ong Yoong Seang/Shutterstock, **22** (top); Maxine Tresize, **12**, **16**; Lauren Turner, Caulfield Grammar, **15** (top & middle); Jill Wilson, **17**; James Wu, **3** (all), **4** (top left & top middle), **5** (top), **6** (top), **8** (all), **10** (top), **13** (top), **14** (bottom), **15** (bottom), **18**, **20** (bottom), **23** (bottom), **24**, **25** (top), **26**, **30** (top).

While every care has been taken to trace and acknowledge copyright, the publisher tenders their apologies for any accidental infringement where copyright has proved untraceable. Where the attempt has been unsuccessful, the publisher welcomes information that would redress the situation.

1 3 5 6 4 2

Contents

Glossary Words

When a word is printed in **bold**, you can look up its meaning in the Glossary on page 31.

Chinese Proverb

Learning is a treasure that will follow its owner everywhere.

China challenges the imagination because of its size. It is big in many ways. It is one of the largest countries on Earth, covering about one-fifth of the continent of Asia. China's population of more than 1.3 billion, or 1,300,000,000, is the world's largest. It has an ancient civilization and a recorded history that date back thousands of years.

A large area of China is covered by tall mountains and wide deserts. Most of the population lives in the fertile lowlands that are bordered by the Pacific Ocean in the east.

The People's Republic of China

Today, China is formally known as the People's Republic of China (P.R.C.). In the last thirty years, the P.R.C. have gone through great social change and the **economy** has grown enormously. China is now one of the United States' major trading partners.

This book looks at China's people, their day-to-day lives, and the cities in which many of them live.

An ancient history

Traditional arts

Very old customs

A country of extremes

A rich variety of wildlife

Plants and medicinal herbs

China's Diverse Peoples

China's people come from fifty-six officially recognized **ethnic groups**. Most of China's population are part of the **Han**. The Han people make up more than 91 percent of the population, which makes them the largest ethnic group both in China and in the rest of the world.

The other peoples in China are usually called the national minorities. Major groups among these are the Zhuang, Uigher, Tibetan, Manchu, and Mongol peoples. These groups come from different parts of Asia. The Uigher are descended from an empire that ruled Mongolia from about 742 CE to 847 CE. Mongolia is a country to the north of China.

China's population

China's population is estimated to be more than 1.3 billion. The population is distributed unevenly across the country. Many more people live in the east of the country, in the rich coastal lands, than in the west where there are deserts and mountains.

The majority of Chinese are part of the Han ethnic group.

The Hani people of Yunnan Province are Tibetan-Burmese in origin.

5

Population Trends

China's population is growing. Many experts think it will peak at about 1.45 billion people in 2030. The population is also aging. This means that the percentage of elderly people in the population is increasing. There has also been an improvement in **life expectancy**, so people are living longer. The introduction of what is known as the "One-Child Policy" has resulted in a sharp drop in the country's birthrate.

China's Growing Population	
Year	Population
1953	582 million
1964	695 million
1982	1.08 billion
1990	1.134 billion
2000	1.266 billion
2007	1.321 billion (estimate)

A group of elderly men playing cards outdoors is a common sight in China.

Did You Know?

Many more boys than girls are born in China. If this trend continues, by 2020 there may be as many as 40 million more men than women of **marriageable age**.

Many Chinese families with only one child have a male child.

China's "One-Child Policy"

China's "One-Child Policy" was introduced as a temporary measure in 1979 to limit the country's population growth. This policy means that sometimes only one child is allowed in a family. If more children are born, the parents must pay an annual fine. The policy is restricted to Han Chinese people living in cities and towns. The government has said it will continue with the policy until at least 2010.

Traditionally, the Chinese have had a cultural preference for male children. This is because they believed that only a male child could continue the **family line**. Also, in the country, males were traditionally expected to work and take care of their parents when their parents were older. This preference has meant that sometimes a female child is not wanted because the family wants its one child to be male.

The Importance Of Family

Chinese people have a long and honored tradition of respecting the old and loving the young.

Until recent times, each Chinese family had a powerful head of family who was in charge of things. The family provided support, security, and other essentials to each individual in it.

Changes in China over the past fifty years have altered the central role of the family. Younger members of the family may need to leave the family to work. The family is still very important to the Chinese, however, and this includes extended family members, such as cousins, aunts, and uncles. Some traditional attitudes remain in China. Marriage and the responsibility of sons to care for their elderly parents are still considered important values in Chinese families.

Often many generations of one family share the same house.

Religion and Beliefs

China is a land of many religions, philosophies, traditions, and beliefs. The main religions are:

- Buddhism
- Taoism
- Islam
- Christianity

Traditions such as *feng shui* are also practiced in China.

Main Religions

Buddhism has been a popular religion in China for more than two thousand years. Christianity is thought to have reached China as early as 400 CE, and Islam came to China in about 600 CE. Taoism and Chinese folk religions, including some that practice **ancestor worship**, are major forms of religion that were founded in China. Taoism and Confucianism began around the same time 2,500 years ago. Confucianism is more a philosophy of life than a religion.

In 2006, the official number of religious followers in China was more than 100 million. The real number may be much higher than this.

People bring offerings to Buddhist shrines.

Buddhist monks shave their heads and wear simple robes.

This Muslim cleric worships at the Niujie Mosque, in Beijing.

Feng Shui

Feng shui is a very old and complex Chinese belief system. It involves the placement and arrangement of objects to achieve harmony within an environment or space, such as a room or garden. *Feng shui* means "wind and water." A place is said to have good *feng shui* if it is thought to be in harmony with nature. Interest in *feng shui* in countries other than China often focuses on applying its principles in homes, offices, and gardens.

A desk that has good *feng shui* is uncluttered.

For Your Information

It is considered good *feng shui* to have a path that has a sharp bend in it. The path should not go straight to the front door. Also, the back door should not be seen from the front doorway. This is because good luck would come in the front door and blow straight out the back door.

A hill was created and two rivers were dug when the Forbidden City was built so that it would have good *feng shui*.

9

Transportation

China's vast population uses many forms of transportation to get from place to place. These include bicycles, boats, planes, trains, cars, camels, and pedicabs.

"Kingdom of Bicycles"

There are several hundred million bicycles in China. The streets are filled with people on bikes.

Not so long ago, swarms of cyclists in the big cities led to China being called the "kingdom of bicycles." Then along came industrial development. The motor car, motorbike, truck, and bus brought freeways, traffic jams, accidents, and pollution. Bicycles became popular again as the roads became gridlocked with traffic. The health, environmental, and cost benefits of this two-wheeled form of transportation have been rediscovered.

Did You Know?

The rickshaw is a two-wheeled cart pulled by a runner. It was once very popular in China. It has now been replaced by a bicycle rickshaw, called a pedicab.

Pedicabs are a convenient way to get around heavy traffic in large Chinese cities.

Bicycles are a popular and cheap way of getting around in China.

Trains

Trains are very important for moving people and goods throughout China. There are more than 5,500 railroad stations around the country. China's railroad system has been called the arteries, or blood vessels, of its economy. In 2006, trains carried more than 7,690 billion pounds (2,870 billion kilograms) of freight and more than 1.26 billion passengers. By 2020, it is expected that there will be 62,000 miles (100,000 kilometers) of railroad track throughout China.

Water Transportation

Water transportation is also a way of traveling in China. The main rivers used for passengers, tourists, and the transportation of goods are the Yangtze and the Pearl rivers. It is possible to navigate through about 3,700 miles (6,000 km) of the Yangtze all year round.

This boat is transporting goods and passengers along the Yangtze River.

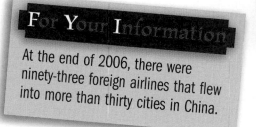

11

Health Care

When the People's Republic of China was founded in 1949, it faced a major health crisis, especially in rural areas. A large number of people had not had access to doctors or hospital treatment for years. There was a high rate of chronic illness.

Health Care for All

The government trained what were known as "barefoot doctors" to help stop the health crisis. Thousands of people were put through brief courses in basic medical matters. They were called "barefoot doctors" because they were often farmers who worked barefoot in their rice fields. These "barefoot doctors" brought health care to the neediest people, who were usually in country areas.

Those days are gone now. A national public health network has been established. Major diseases such as cholera and typhoid have been brought under control, but new lifestyles have seen an increase in cancer and heart disease.

Health costs are expected to rise in China due to the aging population. Older people are more likely to have disabilities and chronic diseases. There will also be a smaller population of working-age citizens to help pay the medical bills.

Did You Know?

Some Chinese are beginning to question traditional medicine. Increasing numbers of Westerners, however, are interested in traditional medicines as an alternative, or at least a complement, to Western health care.

Traditional Medicine

Traditional Chinese medicine is increasingly popular in the **Western** world as well as in China. Traditional Chinese medicine has developed over thousands of years. The theory behind it is that the human body is a "dynamic energy system." Some traditional practices are massage, acupuncture, and the taking of herbal drugs.

Young doctors travel into country areas to test people's blood pressure.

Houses

China's long history and different ethnic groups, climates, and landscapes have meant there is a very diverse range of housing throughout the country. Rural, or country, houses are very different from city houses.

These rural houses are built from local materials and surrounded by stone walls.

Rural Houses

People in rural China live in individual houses or in small settlements where houses are grouped together and surrounded by walls. Houses are sometimes made from stone or brick, but they are more often made from earth and local wood.

City Houses

In the cities, people increasingly live in high-rise apartments. The Chinese government used to allocate housing, called public housing, to city residents as a welfare or employment benefit.
This changed after 1978 when China's government-regulated economy switched to a **market economy**. The public housing became **privatized**. This meant that the government no longer owned the housing, and the private sellers and landlords could decide the prices of houses and rent.

Most people live in high-rise apartments in the big cities.

There is more private ownership of city housing in China than in other countries with more advanced economies. This is a big change in a short time. The government encourages building and there is plenty of demand for housing. Owning their own home is very much the goal of Chinese people these days.

Did You Know?

The original meaning of *hutong* was a place where people lived and gathered together.

Hutongs

A *hutong* is an ancient lane or alley in Beijing. The oldest *hutongs* date back to about 1200 CE. Each one is a unique form of neighborhood.

Some *hutongs* have had only one name since they were built. Some have been declared protected areas because they offer a glimpse of life as it was in Beijing hundreds of years ago.

A *hutong* is a small local neighborhood in the middle of a big city.

Schools

Teaching and learning have been highly valued in China for thousands of years. Today, the government of the People's Republic of China aims for each child to have at least nine years of schooling.

 MEET ## Jiang Huamei

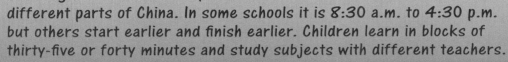

Jiang Huamei is a teacher at a Chinese elementary school in Changzhou, in Jiangsu Province.

In Conversation with Jiang Huamei

Usually the school year starts on September 1 and finishes on June 30. The length of the school day varies in different parts of China. In some schools it is 8:30 a.m. to 4:30 p.m. but others start earlier and finish earlier. Children learn in blocks of thirty-five or forty minutes and study subjects with different teachers.

Most of the children in the class are given a special job to do to help the class run smoothly. Children respect and love their teachers. The bond between teachers and students is very close. Children wear uniforms to school and a red scarf which is a sign of a Young Pioneer.

For Your Information

The Chinese Young Pioneers is an organization for children operated by the Communist Party. There are about 130 million members. You can recognize Young Pioneers by the red scarves around their necks.

Did You Know?

Children in Chinese classrooms do eye exercises for five minutes twice a day. These exercises are to prevent their eyes from becoming too tired.

These schoolchildren in Nanjing practice their eye exercises.

14

Studying in China

Some schools and colleges from around the world have an international **campus** in China. Chinese schools and colleges also accept foreign students. In 2006, more than 160,000 foreign students studied in China.

MEET ## Lauren Turner

Lauren spent time at an international campus in China when she was in ninth grade. Lauren also spent some time in a Chinese classroom.

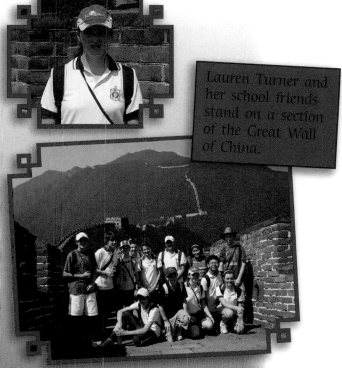

Lauren Turner and her school friends stand on a section of the Great Wall of China.

In Conversation with Lauren Turner

It was really interesting finding out what Chinese students' daily habits are and their priorities. Study is one very high priority in China.

I learned to understand myself better when I was in China and how to be a leader. I realized that I was able to lead and it wasn't quite as hard as I thought it would be.

We were asked to navigate ourselves around Nanjing. We couldn't read the signs or speak fluent Chinese and so I learned a lot about how to lead my fellow students. Now I think I am a more understanding person, a better leader. I am definitely more confident after visiting China.

For Your Information

Learning English as a second language is very popular in China, so many Westerners go to China to work for a year or two as English teachers. More than 150,000 foreign teachers work in China each year.

Students at an international campus in China play sports against local Chinese students.

Language

The Chinese language is thousands of years old. The spoken language has many dialects, or forms, that sound different. A Chinese word sounds different in different dialects, but it looks the same when written. One basic written language is used throughout China.

Spoken Language

Standard Mandarin, also called *Putonghua,* is the official spoken language of the People's Republic of China. Most Chinese people can speak Standard Mandarin. Many Chinese people speak another dialect as well. **Cantonese** is the main dialect used in and around the Special Administrative Region of Hong Kong. It sounds very different from Mandarin.

Written Language

The written Chinese language uses a **pictograph** system, which is made up of signs and symbols. Languages such as English use a phonetic system, which is based on sounds. Written Chinese has more than 50,000 characters. These characters are pictorial and not phonetic, so every word in the language is represented by one character.

Did You Know?

Pinyin is a system that uses Roman letters to represent sounds in Standard Mandarin. *Pin* means "spell" and *yin* means "sound."

The character for "tree" looks like a tree, and the character for "forest" looks like many trees.

木
tree

森
forest

The written language is the same all over China, so posters and billboards can be read by everyone.

Work

As China faces a new era of prosperity, millions of jobs need to be created for its growing population. Work is also needed for people choosing to leave the country and work in the city. These jobs must be created through the development of new industries and businesses.

Heading to the Cities

There are millions of rural Chinese moving from the country to the cities in search of a better life. These people need training and jobs. In the meantime, they do physical work on building sites, water delivery, and garbage removal. These are jobs that are generally not wanted by city people.

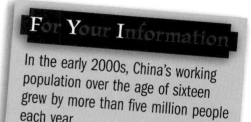

For Your Information

In the early 2000s, China's working population over the age of sixteen grew by more than five million people each year.

MEET Lei Minghua's students

Lei Minghua has been teaching for twenty-five years. He speaks fluent English and teaches at Simao Ethnic Minorities School in Yunnan Province. There are 1,600 students at the school and they come from some of the many peoples in Yunnan: the Wa, Aini, Hani, Dai, and Yi peoples.

These are some of Lei Minghua's student from the Simao Ethnic Minorities School.

In Conversation with Lei Minghua

I see my job as helping students break away from poverty through getting a better education. A good grasp of English will really help them find better jobs.

About one-third of the students at the school are very poor. Many teachers either help students with their studies in their spare time or raise money to buy extra computers for students to use at school. I hope more and more students will go on to college.

Traditional Food

Chinese people love eating. Chinese **cuisine** is eaten at home by 1.3 billion people, and it is a favorite in many other countries, too.

Eating and cooking have a large place in Chinese culture. More than 2,500 years ago, the philosopher Confucius attached great importance to the enjoyment of food and its role in health and wellness.

In all parts of China, a typical meal is made up of a carbohydrate source or starch, such as rice, noodles, pancakes, or buns, as well as dishes such as fish, meat, or vegetables.

Regional Cuisines

There are many distinctive styles of cuisine throughout China.

- The Beijing style features mainly steamed foods, rice buns, and pancakes, as well as steamed rice and, of course, the famous Peking duck.
- The Cantonese style has distinctive stir-fries of meat and vegetables.
- The Szechuan style is very spicy, with meat, fish, and plenty of chilies.

For Your Information

In 1958, the way people in the West said and spelled Chinese names changed when the *pinyin* system was introduced. Mao Tse-tung became known as Mao Zedong and the city of Peking became known as Beijing. This is why the famous Beijing restaurant dish is called Peking duck.

A typical Chinese banquet in a restaurant is served in a number of courses.

Eating a Chinese Meal

Chopsticks and spoons are the basic tools used to eat Chinese meals. Chinese food is cut into bite-sized pieces before it is cooked, so that it may be picked up easily with chopsticks. Each person at a typical Chinese meal gets their own bowl of rice, and selects food from shared plates on the table. Soups and other liquid foods are eaten using a wide, flat-bottomed spoon.

Eating with Chopsticks

Eating with chopsticks for the first time can be very tricky. Learning to use them takes practice, but when you do, it will be fun and easy.

What To Do:

1 Rest the lower chopstick between your thumb and fingers.

2 Grasp the other chopstick like a pencil, between your middle finger and index finger. Hold it in place using your thumb. Once the chopsticks are in this position, the ends of both chopsticks should meet.

3 When picking up food, keep the lower chopstick still. Let the upper one do the work, and use your middle finger to guide it.

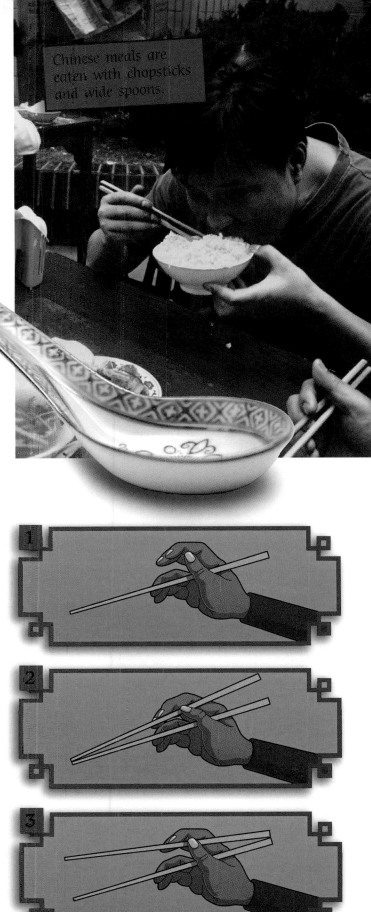

Chinese meals are eaten with chopsticks and wide spoons.

19

China's Favorite Foods

Chinese people enjoy an enormous variety of food. The Chinese pride themselves on the freshness of their ingredients. Almost everything is cooked quickly.

MEET ## Zhang Han Dan

Zhang Han Dan works as a waitress and kitchen assistant at her family's restaurant in Mengma, in Yunnan Province. She has a nine-year-old daughter.

In Conversation with Zhang Han Dan

We opened our restaurant ten months ago. It's near a hot springs resort so we get a lot of customers who are on their way to the resort and also people who work at the local school or for the government. Our restaurant is built out of bamboo and wood and it stands on poles over a large pool.

In China, everyone loves eating fresh food. We grow vegetables for the restaurant in our garden and we catch fish from the pool. Our restaurant is very popular and I am very happy working here.

These waitresses work in a family restaurant.

For Your Information

Traditionally, Chinese people ate all kinds of meat, such as monkey, snake, and turtle. These meats are considered delicacies. As a result, some of these animals have become endangered in China.

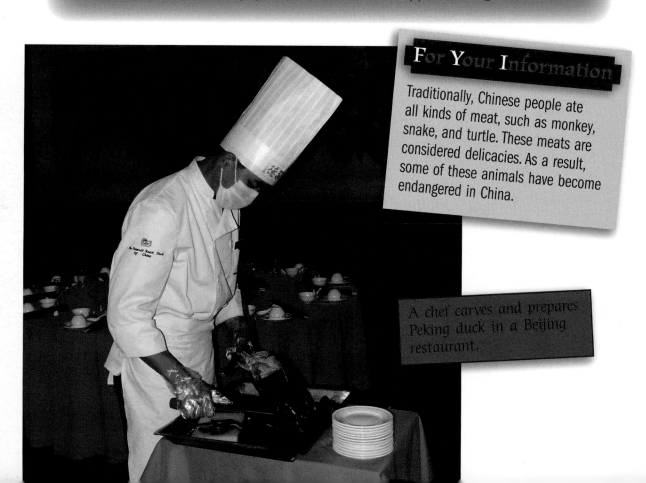

A chef carves and prepares Peking duck in a Beijing restaurant.

20

Rice and Wheat

Most of the starchy foods that are eaten with a meal in China are made from rice or wheat. Rice is prepared in many different forms, such as dumplings and boiled rice. Wheat can be made into different forms, such as noodles and buns.

Forms Of Rice and Wheat

Dumplings
Dumplings are usually **glutinous** rice with pieces of cooked, flavorsome meat inside them. They can be crescent-shaped or small or medium balls.

Rice
There are many different types of rice, such as black and short grain. Rice may be boiled and fairly sticky or fragrant. In southern China, rice can come as fried rice with egg, meat strips, or tiny shrimps.

Noodles
Noodles are made of rice or wheat. They are served fried, boiled, steamed, in soups, or with meat or vegetables.

Buns
Buns are made from wheat. They are usually sweeter than bread. They are often glazed on top. Like dumplings, they may have cooked meat, such as pork, inside them.

Food for Celebration

There are many festivals and celebrations in the Chinese calendar. Special foods are often eaten during particular festivals. Many Chinese foods also have symbolic significance.

Different Chinese dishes are eaten on different occasions.

Special Chinese Foods		
Food	What It Symbolizes	Celebration or Festival
Noodles	Long life	Birthdays
Eggs	Fertility	Birth of a baby
Fruit	Luck and wealth	Chinese New Year
Fish	Prosperity	Banquets and Chinese New Year
Chicken	Unity and family	Weddings and Chinese New Year
Duck	Fidelity	Weddings
Cake	A rich and sweet life	Chinese New Year and Mid-Autumn Festival

Chinese Tea

The Chinese have been drinking tea for thousands of years. **Tea money**, which is cakes or bricks of compressed tea, has been circulating in China since ancient times. China's national drink became very popular during the Tang Dynasty (618 CE–907 CE) and tea shops sprang up in large numbers.

Tea has long played a very important part in the life and culture of the country. Many books and poems have been written about it. The name tea is derived from Chinese words pronounced "tay" and "chah," which may explain the expression "a cup of chah."

Tea for Health and Wellness

At first, tea was valued for its medicinal qualities. It has been known for a very long time that tea helps digestion. Today, it is also thought that drinking tea might contribute to a reduced risk of cancer and heart disease.

Tea is drunk from small, porcelain cups without handles.

Did You Know?

In a traditional Chinese wedding ceremony, the bride and groom kneel before their elders and offer them tea as a mark of respect.

For Your Information

Although there are many types, all tea comes from the same source, the *Camellia sinensis* bush. The way tea leaves are processed accounts for the differences in tea types. The main types are:

- green tea
- black tea
- oolong tea

There are many types of tea available in China and they all have special names.

Where Tea Is Grown

Tea has been grown in China for a long time. It is also grown on plantations in countries such as Indonesia, Sri Lanka, India, and Kenya. Tea is grown in the tropical parts of some countries, such as in South Carolina in the United States.

Chinese tea is prepared and served according to many customs and traditions.

How Tea Is Grown

Tea bushes are usually planted in hedgerows with up to 15,000 bushes per 2.5 acres, or per 100,000 square feet (9,300 square meters). The bushes take up to seven years to mature. Once mature, they may produce tea leaves for one hundred years if looked after carefully. Tea bushes grow best in warm, humid conditions. Differences in climate, soil, and the way the leaf is processed result in up to two thousand types of tea.

Did You Know?

Herbal teas are not considered true teas because they are not made from the *Camellia sinensis* bush.

Tea is grown on large plantations, such as this one in Hubei Province near the Yangtze River.

Cities

Most Chinese people still live in the country but more and more people are moving to the cities. There are more than 150 cities in China with a population of more than 500,000 people. Shanghai is the biggest city in China. It is home to more than 14 million people. The second-largest city is the capital, Beijing. It has more than 10 million people. Other large cities in China are Wuhan, Hong Kong, and the old port city of Tianjin.

Shanghai

Shanghai means "city on the sea." It is modern China's largest and greatest commercial and industrial city. Shanghai's history dates back to between 1000 CE and 1100 CE when it was a fishing village. In the early 1900s, Shanghai was called the "Paris of the East" because of its glamorous style, nightlife, and culture, and its openness to foreign ideas and residents. Shanghai is once again a hot spot in China. Former leader Deng Xiaoping once said, "If China is a dragon then Shanghai is its head."

Did You Know?

San Francisco and Shanghai formed the first China–U.S. sister-city relationship in 1979.

The promenade, or long walkway, alongside the Yangtze in Shanghai is called the Bund.

Beijing

China's capital city, Beijing, is found in the northeast of the country. Beijing has been described as a city facing in two directions. It is a city that is looking back at a rich and historic past, as well as looking forward to a dazzling future. Beijing is where the People's Republic of China was declared in 1949. It is also host to the Olympic Games in 2008.

Beijing is a city built to inspire and impress. Much of the historic Beijing that can still be seen was built during the Ming Dynasty from 1368 CE to 1644 CE. It is crowded with architectural jewels from the nation's **imperial** past, such as the Forbidden City, Summer Palace, Temple of Heaven, and Tiananmen Square.

The Forbidden City in Beijing was built in the early 1400s.

Did You Know?

Before 1958, Beijing was known in the Western world as Peking.

Olympic City

Beijing has been transformed in the last few years. New roads, sporting venues, hotels, and apartment blocks have been built in preparation for the 2008 Olympic Games in Beijing.

The National Stadium in Beijing was constructed for the 2008 Olympic Games.

Famous Landmarks

China's long history and unique culture are visible in its landmarks. Evidence of Chinese inventiveness and artistic skill can be seen in the Great Wall, the Grand Canal, and the historic treasures buried near the city of Xi'an.

The Great Wall of China

The Great Wall of China is the world's longest structure built by humans. It stretches across northern China for about 3,000 miles (5,000 km). To some, it is like a giant stone dragon. Chinese call it the "Ten Thousand Li Wall." *Li* is a Chinese measurement equivalent to about 640 feet (500 m).

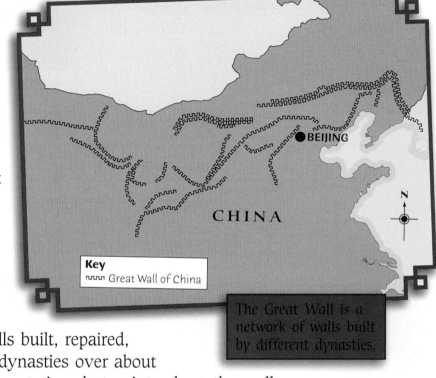

Key
nnnn Great Wall of China

BEIJING

CHINA

N

The Great Wall is a network of walls built by different dynasties.

A Network Of Walls

This great barrier was built as a military defense system. It is made of rocks and earth. The wall is actually a network of walls built, repaired, and extended by many Chinese dynasties over about two thousand years. Soldiers were stationed at points along the wall.

Today, the Great Wall is no longer a defensive barrier. Instead, it is one of China's most popular tourist attractions. This famous wall is sometimes called "the eighth wonder of the world."

Watchtowers along the Great Wall were where troops could shelter, store their weapons, and look out over the country.

The Grand Canal

The Grand Canal of China is the longest canal in the world. It is also the oldest. Work began on the canal 2,500 years ago during the Zhou Dynasty. The Grand Canal extends for more than 1,100 miles (1,770 km), which is longer than the other two great canals of the world, the Suez and Panama canals. The Grand Canal of China stretches from Beijing in the north to Hangzhou, in Zhejiang Province, in the south.

The Grand Canal passes through the ancient town of Wuzheng, in Zhejiang Province.

The Terracotta Army of Xi'an

In 1974, a group of Chinese farmers sunk a well near the city of Xi'an, in Shaanxi Province. This led to the discovery of more than 8 thousand terracotta soldiers, horses, and chariots. These terracotta warriors came from the rule of Emperor Qin Shi Huangdi of the Qin Dynasty, which ruled from 221 BCE until 206 BCE. The emperor ordered the warriors to be made and buried with him. Their discovery is of great cultural and historical importance to China. Like the Great Wall, they have a World Heritage Site listing.

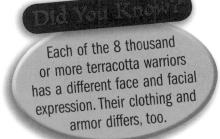

Did You Know?

Each of the 8 thousand or more terracotta warriors has a different face and facial expression. Their clothing and armor differs, too.

Each terracotta warrior is life-size.

27

Sister Cities

Dozens of cities in the United Stages enjoy "sister city" relationships with cities in the People's Republic of China. The idea has been described as a very large version of a "pen pal" exchange in which whole cities are involved, instead of just individuals.

Committees in each sister city arrange student exchanges, business visits, and tours by artists and entertainers. All are designed to deepen understanding and co-operation, one city or community at a time.

The First U.S.–China Sister Cities

San Francisco and Shanghai forged a "friendship" alliance in 1979. It was the first of what are now known as sister city relationships between the United States and China.

Washington, D.C., is the headquarters of an organization called Sister Cities International. This is a nonprofit body that works to create and strengthen partnerships between the United States and international communities. These relationships have also sprung up between United States cities and other countries. They have prospered and enriched the communities they serve.

Shanghai has sister city relationships with many U.S. cities.

San Francisco, California, formed a sister city relationship with Shanghai in 1972.

Chicago, Shenyang, and Shanghai

Chicago, Illinois, established "sister city" agreements with both Shenyang and Shanghai more than twenty years ago. Shenyang is the capital city of Liaoning Province in northeastern China. Shanghai is a major international and trading center on the eastern Chinese coast.

Over the years, these partners have pursued many activities and exchanges in cultural, economic, environmental, and media-related fields. On one occasion, Chicago hosted a course to help train Chinese zookeepers in areas such as visitor education and revenue-producing activities.

Shenyang is a very large industrial city and transport hub.

Phoenix and Chengdu

Every year, many groups and individuals travel between Phoenix, Arizona, and Chengdu as part of the sister city program. Chengdu is the capital of China's Sichuan Province.

In Phoenix, a group called The Chengdu Committee "fosters and encourages mutual understanding, friendship, and a higher quality of life for the people of Phoenix and Chengdu."

Chengdu is an ancient city and is also known as the "panda capital."

A Growing Population

China's people and cities are growing and changing. China's population of more than 1.3 billion people is the world's largest. Most Chinese still live in the country, but there is a big population drift to the cities. There is also a lot of building and development taking place in China, particularly in huge and historic cities, such as Beijing and Shanghai.

With a distinctive culture dating back thousands of years, China is a land of many religions and belief systems. Its people have always prized education. Its unique cuisine and tea are famous around the world. As China's population and cities grow, its influence on the world grows, too.

The lion is a symbol of Chinese New Year all around the world.

Shanghai is China's busiest city!

A teacher on a study tour shares a joke with Hani women in Yunnan Province.

Glossary

ancestor worship	the ancient belief that people who have died can help the living and should be worshipped
campus	the grounds of a school or college
Cantonese	the Chinese dialect spoken in southern China and Hong Kong
cuisine	a style of cooking
economy	the finances of a country
ethnic groups	groups of people that have common, recognizable cultures
family line	the line of descent of a family
feng shui	an ancient belief system aimed at achieving harmony with the environment
glutinous	sticky or gluey
Han	the largest ethnic group in China
imperial	connected with an empire
life expectancy	the age to which a person will probably live
market economy	where buyers and sellers, not the government or officials, decide the price of things
marriageable age	between twenty and forty-five years old
pictograph	a picture symbol for a word or phrase
privatized	switched from government control to private ownership
tea money	cakes or bricks of compressed tea that are used as a form of currency
Western	related to the parts of the developed world that are not covered by eastern Asia

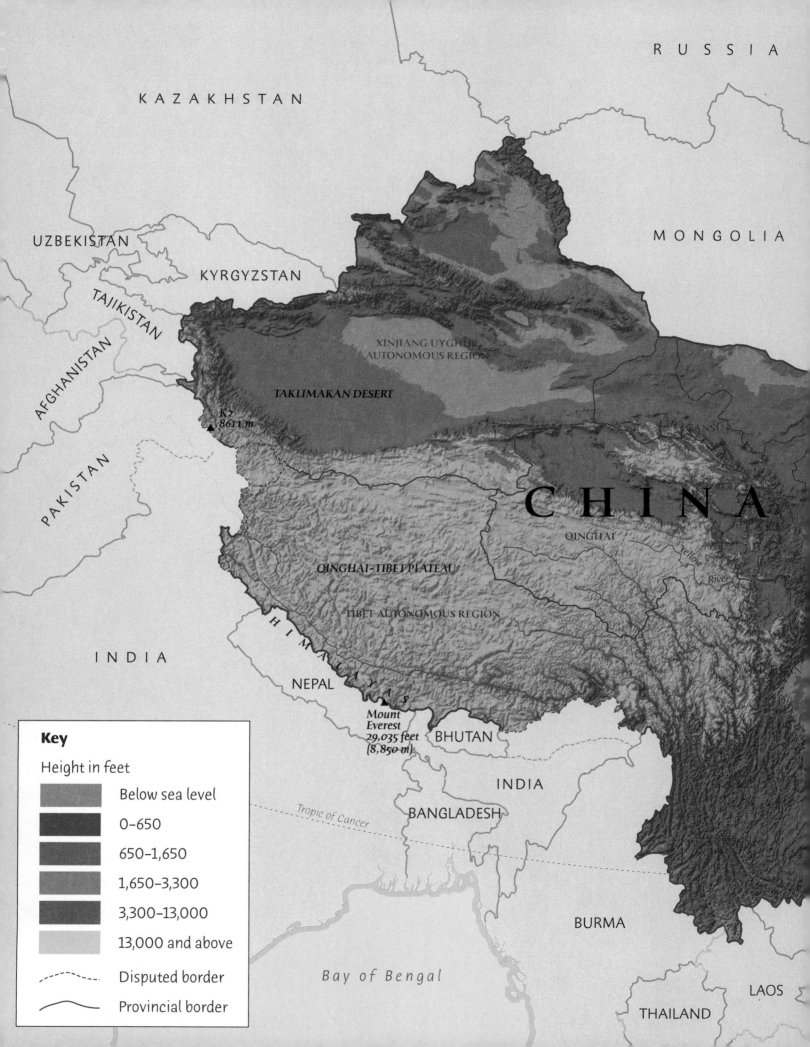

RUSSIA

KAZAKHSTAN

UZBEKISTAN

KYRGYZSTAN

MONGOLIA

TAJIKISTAN

AFGHANISTAN

XINJIANG UYGHUR
AUTONOMOUS REGION

TAKLIMAKAN DESERT

GANSU

PAKISTAN

▲ K2
8611 m

CHINA

QINGHAI

Yellow
River

QINGHAI-TIBET PLATEAU

INDIA

TIBET AUTONOMOUS REGION

HIMALAYAS

NEPAL

▲ Mount
Everest
29,035 feet
(8,850 m)

BHUTAN

INDIA

BANGLADESH

Tropic of Cancer

Key

Height in feet

Below sea level

0–650

650–1,650

1,650–3,300

3,300–13,000

13,000 and above

- - - - Disputed border

‿‿‿ Provincial border

BURMA

Bay of Bengal

LAOS

THAILAND